# Resilient

## MY STORY, MY WAY, MY TIME

# JASMINE WRIGHT

## Disclaimer

Resilient is a personal reflection on experiences and insights shared for inspirational purposes. The author is not a licensed therapist, counselor, or mental health professional, and the information presented in this book is based solely on their personal journey. While the author advocates for therapy as a valuable resource, this book should not be considered a substitute for professional mental health treatment. Readers are encouraged to seek guidance from a qualified therapist or counselor for individual advice tailored to their personal needs. Additionally, certain characters and situations described in Resilient have been modified or fictionalized to respect the privacy of those involved. Any resemblance to actual persons, living or deceased, or to actual events is purely coincidental.

# Dedication

This book is dedicated to my daughter Khori. I want you to always know that you were destined to be here. Anytime you go through any difficult situations in life, know that you have purpose. You fought so hard to be here. I am excited to watch you grow up and I pray that God allows me to witness who He called you to be because I already know you are someone special. You are my everything. I thank God daily for you. I love you, my miracle child.

# Table of Contents

# Chapter One

## Ghosted from the Beginning

The night was one of those nights where I had no intentions of going anywhere. The guy I was currently dating was not acting right, and when a girl is dealing with her emotions, it is kind of best not to be around people. I never desire to bring the vibe down, so my intentions were to stay in. My friend would not let up though. She insisted on us at least going downtown. I still did not want to, but I decided to accompany her and try to be in the best mood possible. She understood the situation though and didn't pressure me about my mood.

As we ended our night, I felt kind of good about getting out and not letting my former relationship steal the enjoyment from me. As we stood by my car and talked, two guys walked up. I was familiar with one of them, he was a friend from church, so I greeted him with a smile and a hug. As he and I continued to talk and catch up, my friend was in conversation with his friend whom I did not know. I did hear him ask me if I was married, I wasn't of course, but I was in no mood for any dude. I had just ended a relationship and did not want to go there.

As my friend and I got in the car to leave she reported that she had given this guy my number. I was like "Oh goodness!" Again, I was not in the mood, but I laughed it off. I loved my friend and I know she meant well. The very next day he texted me. By then, the end of my other relationship had taken place so I welcomed the text, a little. We started to text back and forth, getting to know each other better. His name was Rodrick, and he recently moved back to the area. He was nice and comical, and I loved to laugh. I was also glad to know he knew the Lord. That was important to me. As I waited for the other shoe to fall off, as it always does with dudes, it did: He told me he was going through a divorce, and it was "almost final." I had heard this story too many times, and it sounded like a broken record. I instantly became uninterested.

The following Monday, we were still texting, and he asked me to come by his job. At the job, he told me that the divorce had been made final, and he was happy to report it. I was in shock because like I said, that hardly ever happens.

From that point, I was looking forward to continuing to get to know him. So far, he was funny, cool, honest, and hardworking. I started to feel immediately safe with him, and now that he was divorced, we could really take it somewhere. I felt great, at least until he ghosted me.

# Chapter Two

## Zebra Stripes

For two weeks I didn't hear anything from this man. Not even a text. I wondered what had happened, what had I said wrong, had he gotten back with his ex? When someone ghosts you, you are kind of left to decide on your own what happens, and even overthink the whole situation. It's a cruel and unfair act and sadly people do it every day. It didn't hurt much because I was still getting to know him, but I wished I knew why. Then, one day, just as it can happen after being ghosted, I received a text. I immediately asked him where he had been, and he explained that the divorce had brought some emotional trauma, and he had to deal with those things. I sympathized with that. Break-ups bring on emotional trauma so of course a divorce can do that. I forgave him, although I had some reluctance, I figured I had never walked in his shoes, so I needed to be understanding about it.

We officially began dating and spending time together. He did have a child from his previous marriage. As we began dating, she knew me as daddy's friend which worked okay for us. We didn't want her involved too fast, as we cared about her emotions as well in the aftermath of the divorce. We would take her to the movies with us and on little family date nights. She called me Miss Jasmine, which I always thought was cute and respectful. Rodrick loved to date and go out of town. I loved those things as well, so it fit. I admit, looking back, things moved super-fast with us. Before I knew it, the dating was consistent, his daughter was with us on a regular basis, and we were meeting each other's family. I remember the first time I met his mom; she warned me about a few things about him. She was laughing as she told me these things, so I laughed along with her. In the midst of her saying all these things, I knew she loved her son, and if push came to shove, she would have his back. I believe she liked me from the start, but there was something being held back. I could feel it. She could not fully love me.

I was becoming so content in our relationship. He was spending time at my apartment and being so sweet. One day though, we were at my place, and I was preparing a meal for us. Within the conversation, we began to bicker, and the bickering escalated to a full-out argument. It got so bad that he blew up at me and stormed out of the apartment. I was in shock. I had no idea how things had escalated that fast, and why he left like that. My emotions were all over the place. He returned thirty minutes later apologizing. He was so sorry and hurt by his own actions. I had never seen a man apologize and admit his wrong like that. I was so confused, but I accepted his apology.

As time progressed in our relationship, I noticed he would argue a lot with his ex-wife. He would get so frustrated about it, but I did my best to be his peace. I knew he was under a lot of stress because he was now living with his mom, and she gave him only six months to find a place. Lucky for him he didn't have a ton of bills so she figured he could save. We would talk for hours about marriage and what life would be like if we were. Rodrick was a few years older than me, so I understood that he wanted marriage and stability.

At times his mom would apply pressure about him moving out and it would hurt him. He would cry and begin to call himself a failure. I would feel so bad for him and could not understand how his mom did not see he was trying. Although he had very little bills, he just did not have the money. He and I spent so much time together, that he began to notice when I would buy myself expensive things, especially for my workouts. I bought a pair of BEATS, and he sadly mentioned he wanted a pair and could pay me for them later. I made the purchase on my credit card because I understood that sometimes you want something nice. The strange thing to me was that when I would ask him about the payment which would be coming due, he always made an excuse, that led to me asking a question, which normally ended in us having a huge argument.

# Chapter Three

## Love is Hard, Right?

By now everyone knew we were a couple; his family, my family, and our friends. I would consistently visit him at his job and have regular conversations with his co-workers. On one such visit, somehow the conversation went into discussing credentials, and it came up that Rodrick did not have a degree. I was sure I remembered him telling me he graduated from the same college I had so I was very confused. I began to ask him about it to verify, and he assured me that he only told me he attended school, not graduated from a college. I continued to press the issue a bit because I knew what he told me. This soon turned into me making him feel beneath me. He said I always thought I was better than him, and it was only a matter of time before this came out. I felt so bad because I never wanted him to feel that way. I loved this man, and I respected him as my man. I did my best to convince him I did not feel that way, and we finally made up.

Our relationship was so much fun. The dates were continuous, and always to the best places with the best food and entertainment. It felt good to have a man who would take me out and wasn't afraid to be caught up in anything. I trusted him so much. The vacations were even better. We would plan trips and head out of town. We also found fun things to do. We were making memories, and our laughter together was amazing. I lived for the good times because there were times when things got bad. Most times the bad times were prefaced by an argument with his ex-wife. They would get into terrible arguments and screaming matches, and then all of a sudden, he would become angry at me. I never understood what I did wrong, but he would say he was no good for me, and talking to her made him see it. He would then threaten to break up with me. I would cry and try to convince him that there was nothing wrong with our relationship and that his issues with her had nothing to do with us, but he was not hearing it most of the time. He would find something wrong and let me go.

After the arguments, he would block me. I could not even contact him to try to talk it out. I would hurt for days. I could not understand how the man who loved me, dated me, vacationed with me, and shared so many amazing moments could do this to me. I did all I could to cope because I could not reach him during these times. This toxic routine continued over and over, and I felt that I was losing myself each time. Although this only normally went on for a week, it felt like a month. We would almost always run into each other at the gym, and he would then unblock me and text me. I would share with my friends what was going on with us, and they understood. They never judged me for the madness, and I was grateful to have sisters in Christ like that.

As stated, the texting and unblocking normally happened after he saw me at the gym. He knew how to apologize and make me feel so loved. After he expressed his feelings and explained the issues I would always understand. I felt like I had not walked in his shoes, so I had no right to tell him how to feel. I needed to be his peaceful and understanding girlfriend. By now I had hopes of being his wife. I loved and cared for him so much. As our relationship continued into a new year, things remained the same: fun, trips, laughter, arguments, breakups, and then the cycle would continue. It was so toxic, but somehow, I felt that these rough days were going to lead to better days. I had faith in this, and I believed that we could get through it. These were just growing pains. Everyone goes through those, what makes us any different?

# Chapter Four

## A Bride to NOT Be

Strange enough, as much time as we spent together I had never officially met Rodrick's ex-wife. She knew about me and saw me at events concerning the child, but no one introduced us. We didn't have any issues either. In each other's presence, we were there, and that's what mattered. There was one time I was at his mom's house, and he told me his ex-wife wanted to talk to me. I headed to meet her, but his mom stopped me. She told me I did not have to go outside to talk to her, and I could go back. I thought that was so weird, but I did not question it. I figured maybe she just wanted to meet me, but his mom didn't want the negativity in the home. I let it go.

As we got into the new year, I knew it was time for Rodrick to get out of his mom's home. We had a special date night coming up and I knew we would spend a ton of time together, and I planned to take his mind off all of the stress of having to move out soon. We went out to celebrate the day, and during the conversation he kept saying "if" we ever get married. I started to get irritated about the comment, because I knew I wanted to marry him, and I hated hearing him speak as if it was unlikely in any way. I was so bothered by it. He had all but promised to marry me one day, so I did not want to hear anything like this. I had given this man my ring size months ago, in hopes that a ring was coming. When we arrived home, I went in the kitchen and began straightening up. As I turned around to see if he was listening to me while I talked, he was on one knee asking for my hand in marriage.

I was in shock. He really proposed, and he really wanted to marry me. He could not have asked on a more perfect day. I cried and he cried, and we expressed our love. After we announced our engagement to our parents, they shared in our excitement, but his mom made a comment that was strange. She told us that Rodrick's ex-wife sent her a "thanks for the heads up." I knew she was referencing our engagement, and I thought it was strange that Rodrick did not tell her, but I brushed it off as maybe he was being selective about who he told. Our focus now was saving money for a wedding, so we knew we needed to consolidate as soon as possible. We spent more time together, but

Rodrick did not officially move in. We started booking venues and making preparations for our wedding day. I was so excited. I needed my wedding to be perfect. It needed to be everything I could ever dream of. Rodrick was supportive and he wanted the day to be a dream for me as well. I loved him even more for that.

In the midst of our planning, we still made time to date and spend time together. One night while at the movies all snuggled up, I noticed he kept getting a facetime call. I asked him who was calling and he explained that I knew who she was and it was no big deal. I accepted what he said in the moment, but I also peeped at the phone and made a mental note of her name. When I got the opportunity, I looked her up on Facebook, but she did not look familiar to me at all. As I sat there I had the certain urge to search his Facebook account. I knew that if he thought I somehow knew this girl based on my Facebook page, he had to have initially talked to her on Facebook. I needed to get into his account, and the gag was, I knew the password because I created the account.

As I logged into his account, my heart was racing. My woman's intuition was heating up. I knew something was wrong, but Lord knows I did not want it to be. I checked the messages and what I saw caused my chest to hurt. The message between him and several women got worse as I continued to read. One woman he was having deep conversations with. Here I was planning a wedding, and this man was communicating with women as if he was single. I was floored, heartbroken, and fuming.

# Chapter Five

## I Do

I did what most women would do in this situation and reached out to this woman. I wanted to know if she knew about me and how long this had been going on. Tears were in my eyes as I thought about how my parents were working overtime and cutting back to ensure we had everything we needed for our wedding. The woman began to tell me everything I wanted to know and even proclaimed to love Rodrick. There was so much information and some of it I didn't even want to know. I was hurting so bad. I could not wait to confront Rodrick. When I did, he attempted to blow up at me about going into his account and contacting her, but I was not letting up. I laid into him heavy and let him know I was not continuing the wedding planning, and I deserved answers. He finally gave in and admitted everything.

Rodrick took responsibility for it all. He was sorry, but this time I was not sure if that was going to be good enough.

I knew the truth about everything. I proceeded to call both of our parents to tell them everything that was going on. My mother was devastated, and her heart broke for me. I hated to hear her disappointment. His mom was upset as well, but she kept asking who the woman was. I told her, and she became shocked as if she knew the woman. I asked her about it, and she said she was familiar with her. In that moment, I was almost sure I did not want to get married anymore. This woman and him had a history I could not compete with. Before the conversation ended his mom told me not to marry him.

As the days went on I was deeply depressed. I was also dealing with Rodrick apologizing every hour, and notifications that there were meetings we needed to attend pertaining to the wedding. I was miserable. I could not bring myself to cancel the meetings. As much as I hated Rodrick, I loved him the same. I managed to get myself together to attend the meetings. I plowed through them with tears in my eyes pretending to be a happy bride. After each meeting and even before them, I would talk to Rodrick and he would cry and cry plus beg, as he continued to confess everything he ever did to me. He began doing everything I asked him to do and more. He cleared out all of those messages and blocked the women. He even gave me access to his phone and accounts. He catered to me day and night.

One day Rodrick came to me and asked if we could go to counseling. He expressed his love once again and told me he could not lose me. I was pleased with this as much as I still hurt. Rodrick was a changed man as far as I could see. All of the toxic behavior ceased. There was no more arguing. He barely raised his voice or asked anything of me. I started to see that maybe those were just growing pains, and maybe we just needed to pass the hardest test which was the current one. I loved having my way and whatever I said it was "okay baby." I continued to check his phone and accounts and found no evidence of wrongdoing at all. He had completely gotten rid of the woman who he had been communicating with. Rodrick became everything a woman could dream of, and I decided I was ready to pledge my life to him.

# Chapter Six

# What the?

Rodrick and I began premarital counseling. Life was so good. We both talked about the insecurities that we were bringing into the marriage and talked about how we could work through those. Rodrick was still so agreeable and sweet. We continued to date on the regular. Everything improved with us. We continued our wedding planning. All of the dates were still on, and we were well on our way to marriage. Rodrick could not have been more perfect, and there was not a slip-up in sight.

The week of the wedding Rodrick had a car accident. I was so grateful that his life was spared, but it did take us down to one vehicle. He was loaned a temporary car, and we were grateful for that. I decided we would move into a bigger apartment to accommodate his child. One night while we were getting settled Rodrick came into the house with a huge flat-screen television. I was glad he was contributing to the entertainment in our home. The week of the wedding was so exciting, and Rodrick was being so romantic. He was loving and kind. He was my protector, and he was just there.

The wedding day arrived, and everything flowed perfectly. We got to spend time with everyone. They were all so happy for us. While on the honeymoon we began having an amazing time, as we always did when we traveled. One night at dinner though, I noticed he was texting and seemed to get frustrated. I knew that when this happened, he was normally texting his child's mom, and I quickly let him know that this time was about us, and I needed his full attention. Whatever that was about could wait. He explained that she was asking about buying clothes. I felt that that was so mundane and out of order. It was our honeymoon. We got over that small spat and began to focus on us.

We enjoyed the rest of our trip and made some pretty cool friends. We were looking forward to our new life. Everything continued to go smoothly. We were able to get Rodrick a new car, and we established our routines. As we progressed as newlyweds, Rodrick began preparing for his annual trip with his friends. I was okay with it, although we were very new to marriage. While there he and I remained in constant contact, so I did not feel any way about it. At least until he sent me a picture with a girl in it blowing kisses at the camera.

# Chapter Seven

# Furious

I did not know Rodrick or his friends would be around women on the trip, and I guess I was naïve not to think so. I was so mad at Rodrick, and I began addressing my feelings immediately. He tried to explain that their rooms were booked incorrectly, and they ended up sharing a balcony with a group of women. He said he was on the balcony and the young lady got in the camera. I was still mad, and that excuse did not work for me. Plus, I still did not understand why he sent it to me. He claimed I was blowing things out of proportion.

The next day, Rodrick called and explained that he was sorry. One of his homeboys told him he was wrong, and he understood it better. I appreciated that, but I really just needed him to get home and be alone with me. Once he was home, we were able to get over all of that and move forward. Things continued to go well until our finances became very strained. One day I looked up and realized I was paying most of the bills: rent, cell phones, car insurance, and more. I knew child support had become very demanding for Rodrick, but I could not figure out why I was so burdened.

After I began to try to evaluate things, I realized that Rodrick was not working as hard on his job. When I tried to talk with him about the money issues, he encouraged the fact that both of our incomes were our income, so it did not matter who paid what. I heard what he was saying, but I knew if I did not come up with the money, we would fail at something. I began to take on more clients, even working weekends if need be. I was beyond stressed, and I tried to brainstorm with Rodrick about ways he could make money. He always told me he could not get a part-time job, because that would take time away from him and his daughter. I was not a parent, so I accepted that reasoning.

It began to get to the point where I was unable to keep myself up. I was unable to buy some of the things I wanted or wanted to wear. The debts began to pile up fast. Rodrick had expensive taste and was somehow able to acquire the things he wanted. At this point, as I began to look around it became clear that Rodrick did not have my back on this. The support he had once promised me was no longer there. Every time I addressed the issue, he continued to say it was "our" money. Aside from that he would lay down the pity party and make me feel worse for even bringing up our issues.

As all of this continued, our accounts continued to decrease. I started to question who I married. I felt destitute. I was making sure I did not get pregnant. We barely had money; I knew a baby would add to the stress. While I was working on the weekends, Rodrick was enjoying life and going to football games in his fancy clothes. One night while I was going over the phone bill, I saw a number showing up a little too frequently. I realized that this was the girl who was FaceTiming Rodrick that night at the movies all those months ago. I called the number and left a very nasty message on her voicemail. She knew we were married. When Rodrick arrived home, I confronted him, and he responded, "It does not matter who I talk to." I was furious.

# Chapter Eight

## Separate but Married

Rodrick showed me that night that he had not changed at all. I was so broken. I moved into the guest room. We were literally existing in the same space from that night forward. We did not talk unless it pertained to the simplest things: food, bills, his daughter, etc. We were beefing in our own home. Per usual he blocked me on his cell phone. This was nothing new because I experienced that all through dating, although I was sure all of that was over once we were married. He showed me a totally new person, but now he was showing his "true colors" as they say. I was so lonely in our home, so I reached out to a mutual friend of ours. She told me she would call and talk to him, which she did. He told her he would talk to me, and that we were going to work through it all, but when he would come home, he would say nothing to me. It was as if he put on a different face for certain people, but I saw the real him.

It was so quiet in our home it was sickening. We had a television in the bedroom and at times we would watch it together, but no words would exchange, and at the end of the night, I would return to the guest room. One night out of nowhere, he finally apologized. All I could do was ask him why he was still talking to this girl months later, after all of the damage this caused. I told him we needed to go back to counseling. I was relieved that he agreed, but I was not at peace about it. In counseling the counselor explained that it did not matter if the girl was a friend or not. She had to go. She was bringing so many issues into our marriage which is what mattered. He finally agreed to let her go once again.

After attending therapy, and being satisfied with Rodrick letting this girl go, I moved back into the bedroom with my husband. Things began to improve, and we worked on having a loving marriage. I eased back into some things with him. It was so hard for me to trust him at all. I began looking at his followers. I saw where he was liking pictures of IG models. He was even commenting on some of the pictures. These pictures had him mesmerized and it was obvious. I was hurt and exhausted because we had discussed all of this in counseling, and he was no longer supposed to be engaging at all with anyone. At this point, I decided to go to the phone records again, and once again I saw that he had been texting two girls we had issues with before.

I distinctly remembered Rodrick clearing out these women, so it was clear that he added them all back. I could not see what those texts were of course, so I reached out to one of the young ladies, and she assured me that there was nothing wrong and they were just friends. The problem was he didn't even need to be reaching out because they were old relationships. I was so tired, and it was close to the holidays. I confronted him, and once again he asked me to stop checking his social media and phone records. He told me if I stopped checking, I would not know anything. I was disgusted, and I moved out of the room again.

# Chapter Nine

## Last Time

I Told Rodrick I needed a divorce. I was one exhausted woman. The situation with the bills was still the same, and we were going into a new season with all of this drama. Rodrick had become straight-up unlikable. He was not the man I thought he was at all. Deep down, I knew this for a while. All of the things he told me about his ex-wife were lies. The level of deception he used on people was ridiculous.

We remained in the apartment together, but I continued to sleep in the guest room. Our conversation was once again the bare minimum. I was mentally checked out of this marriage. One day while at church during altar prayer, Rodrick dropped to his knees and began crying his eyes out. I looked at him in disgust. He was crying as if he wanted to save his family. In front of these people, it seemed he had a heart of gold. I left him there at the altar, while his friend came and helped him up. His mom meanwhile was praising the Lord as if her son had found God. It was all disgusting.

Rodrick and I rode to church separately most Sundays. We continued to ride separately during our in-house separation. He decided though after "finding Christ" he wanted to talk about our marriage. I was done with him. Everything he said, and was going to say, was a lie. Although our marriage was dying before us, at times he acted as if he didn't even know. It was sad what we were going through each day.

At the start of the new year, his daughter got her phone taken away, so Rodrick gave her his old phone to use for an alarm. One day the phone was left in her bedroom, and I decided to pick it up and look at the messages. I began to read the messages between him and his ex-wife. There were messages that dated back to when we were dating. He was asking her if they could be together, and she was telling him "no." This man was asking to work things out with his ex, right before he proposed to me. There were other messages from even earlier in our relationship where he wanted to be with her, but she refused him. I became so angry once again, and I was tired of being angry.

I reached out to Rodrick, and once again told him what I knew. I explained that I understood that he never wanted to marry me. I told him I saw that he had to clear it with her before he could propose to me. I knew he was at work, but I had to let him know what I knew. He continued to tell me that I needed to stop looking for things. Once again, he took no accountability for his actions. He began to profess his love for me and how he did not want her, because he had his wife. The more he talked the more I wanted a divorce. I was so done with this man.

Once I began to open up about my marriage ending so soon, people began to tell me we needed to work it out. I did not want to hear anything. I appreciated people rooting for my marriage to work, but I was done with mine. I did not want to do this, but between the people begging, and Rodrick begging, plus agreeing to go to counseling, again, I gave in and decided to give it one more try.

# Chapter Ten

## I Needed My Mom

Rodrick and I started going to counseling again, but this time everything came to a halt. During this time neither one of us could work. Things were looking grim for us in an already financially strained household. Rodrick's mom suggested that we move in with her, pay off our debt, save money, and eventually build a home of our own. I was not sold on this idea at all. His mom seemed to be a bit controlling, and I could not see myself being a grown woman and wife co-existing with her. Rodrick desired to make this move. He asked me to allow him to be the man and trust the decision and the process. We were able to get out of our lease, so he felt this was the perfect plan for us. I reluctantly agreed to it.

We moved in with his mom, and I admit I did not like it from the start. His mom began advising us on what to do with money and what we should not do with it. Rodrick would repeat everything his mom said and wanted us to always do things exactly how she wanted. I hated it and this only intensified the friction we already had. I began sleeping in a different room there. We would watch movies, play video games, and work out. His mom cooked every day so that worked out. The best part about this season was we were paying off our debts. We only kept a small amount of spending money. His daughter would come visit us, and thus gave her mom a break which I am sure she needed.

As time progressed in isolation, Rodrick began to talk about people he heard from, from his job. He was giving their updates on their lives. These check-ins triggered me because these people were not his friends, so I did not understand why I needed an update on them. I asked him why he felt the need to check on people after he mentioned a familiar name one day. Once I looked into it, I realized he and this girl had prior conversations. He started to play the check-ins off like these people were asking about me when in reality these were his exes. He wanted me to be at ease when I saw the people show up on his phone. I was so angry at him for once again disregarding his vows for these women.

Rodrick and I begin having full-blown arguments in his mom's house. He kept telling me I needed to stop looking for things. During most of our arguments I don't think his mom heard, but one night she did. She was standing in the hall looking at us. I was screaming "I am done!" Rodrick began saying he was done too. He would add hurtful comments like how he never wanted kids with me, or a house. His mom interrupted the argument and asked me to come to her room to talk. I had begun packing my bags to leave by this time. I needed to go to my mom's house, and I needed a moment to breathe. I was crying in his mom's face, repeatedly telling her what I needed. She kept telling me to go back to my room and not to leave. I explained to her that I needed my mom's support, and that I just needed to go. I grabbed my things and left to go to my mom's house a few towns over. I cried the entire night.

# Chapter Eleven

## Can't Keep A Good Woman Down

By this time, I had begun working again in the beauty industry. I would have to get up early in the morning to drive back to town to meet with my clients. The crying the night before did me some good because I had gathered enough strength to call Rodrick's mom to let her know I was on my way back up the road. She informed me that I could no longer stay in her home and that me and Rodrick needed to work on our marriage apart from each other. I was blown away by her response. I explained to her that I actually never wanted to come to her home, but she insisted and that's why we were there. Furthermore, how was she going to house my husband and not me? I was speechless. I ended the conversation and thought about the fact that I had no money to even get another place because we had used all of our money to pay off our debts. I felt so destitute and lost. This was a woman, putting another woman out on the street.

I finally called Rodrick, and his response cut even deeper. He said, "Well if my mama said that, then that's what it is. You are no longer welcome." I was dizzy. This was the same man who asked me to trust him to make the decision to move to his mom's house. This was most certainly not my husband. Our marriage was officially over. I called my parents to let them know what was happening. I hated to even place my issues on them, but they were my lifeline, and I needed them to know. They were beyond upset about this. They could not understand how my husband, a raised-in-the-church man, a man who was supposed to be the head of his household, allowed his mom to control our marriage. That night I went back to my mom's house.

For about a week and a half I stayed with my mom. I did not have time to feel sorry for my situation because I needed to resolve it and get things done. In the meantime, I was looking for divorce attorneys and trying to find somewhere to live. I knew I did not want to live in another apartment. This was the decision we made after the last apartment, so why should I change my desires because of my circumstances? I began looking at houses. I already had a realtor, and she was still advising me. Within two weeks of being destitute, basically put out on the street, and abandoned by my husband, I alone was approved for a brand-new home and began the contract to build. My dad was able to find me a studio to stay in to cut down my drive, until my home was built.

# Chapter Twelve

## Life Lessons

As I prepared myself to move into the studio apartment, I realized I had nothing to start with. All of our items were collectively in a storage unit, and with us being married, nothing was solely mine. So here I was starting from square one. My dad saw how much all of this pained me, as did my mom, so they were able to buy me a few items to survive. I slept on an air mattress. I chose not to furnish the studio completely because I felt it would be a waste. Some friends of our family, Mr. and Mrs. Crenshaw knew about my situation and stepped in to bring food and other necessities. All of this reassured me that even when you are an adult, or married even, a village is still necessary. We never know where life will take us, and sometimes, we have to pull ourselves up from rock bottom.

I did not have any money for real, so my dad was signing up for pretty much everything and continuously helping out.

I was researching lawyers and I found a few, but I would need to be able to pay them. I had no idea how I would come up with this money, and I knew Rodrick did not care. I felt so stuck, but then my dad saw the pain it caused me, and one day he handed me the money to pay for my divorce. I cried so hard. The man who had given me away to a man we thought we could trust was now, like the perfect father he was, handing me my freedom from this man who mishandled me. I was so grateful to him. I hired the attorney and gave her all of the information. She proceeded to contact Rodrick.

Once Rodrick was contacted by the lawyer, he called me. He wanted to know why an attorney was calling him. I was speechless, but since he wanted it to be this way, I explained to him that I was filing for divorce. He proceeded to say threatening things to me. He told me he was contesting the divorce, and he would force me to spend a ton of money on the process. He told me he did not understand why we were getting a divorce, that he was under the impression this was a temporary separation, and we would soon get back together. At that point, I got dizzy. I had been put out on the street by him and his mom and he thought this was a game.

I ended the conversation with Rodrick because it wasn't going anywhere, and I proceeded to let his ex-wife know we were getting divorced. I also shared with her how Rodrick thought we were in a temporary situation. She explained that she had been through the same thing. They would have these huge disagreements, separate, and then he would come back when he got ready. This was all normal behavior for him, but it was not marriage for me. This was not going to be my normal. A husband should be in his home, not in and out of it. The legal proceedings began, and I found out Rodrick wanted to leave all of our debts to me. Per usual.

We had only a few debts and they were mainly things we both wanted and had purchased together, but he declared in the divorce that they belonged to me solely. Everything he did during this process was hurtful. Although he left the debts to me, he also wanted the items I had to pay for. I was so exhausted with him and sad. My house was coming along so I looked forward to that, but fighting with him was killing my spirit. Any way he could get over and gain favor he was trying it within this divorce. I learned so many valuable things in this process, one being if a person can't get something on their own credit without being married, don't go in with them to get it, especially if they are irresponsible. Absolutely no co-signing, unless you know they can pay for it. I know spouses are in this together, and I may sound harsh, but take it from someone who knows: if your credit and name is all that the marriage can rely on, and you have decided to be with this person, be leery when they are comfortable using your credit and uninterested in building theirs.

# Chapter Thirteen

## Sweet Success

In some good news, the divorce did remain uncontested, but to my disappointment, my builders got behind on my house. I was so hurt. I began to think that God was telling me divorce was not the answer. I knew what the Bible said, and it said "God hates divorce." Here I was in the middle of what God hates asking Him to bless me. This made no sense. Maybe I had moved too fast, maybe Rodrick needed another chance. I began to pray, and I told God I needed a sign. I told him that if I rode by my house and they were not working on it, then I would not sign the divorce papers, and reconsider what I was doing. I was so nervous getting in my car that day, my heart was skipping beats, but I knew what I told God and I would honor Him either way. As I turned on the street into what was to be my new neighborhood my stomach was in knots. As I pulled up to my address, my eyes began to water. There were those men working diligently to get my house built! I cried so hard and screamed, "Glory to God!" I then put petal to the metal to sign those papers.

Upon arriving to sign the divorce papers I found out Rodrick had already signed. This was such a relief. A little while after the signing, Rodrick still reached out to ask if we could work it out. We had two weeks to reverse the entire ordeal, and he knew to reach out within that time. I told him no. He began to cry and beg and he explained that it was so hard for him to stop thinking of me. He even promised me that his mom would no longer be involved in our marriage. There was no way I was going to allow Rodrick back into my life to hurt me again. All the while I listened to him, I knew this. The damage that was done, could not be reconciled. I ended the conversation.

Going forward Rodrick continued to pick at me. Other times he would send messages about how I never liked him, and he knew it. We only had a small amount of business left between us. Once we were done with this final piece, I blocked Rodrick on many of the platforms where he contacted me. My life was at peace, and it felt so good without him in it. I began smiling more, and I was so much happier. I decided I wanted to focus on my business and rebrand. I was a new person. My fitness even became a priority again. I finally moved into my brand-new home, and shortly after that I purchased a new car, and began planning trips with my family. I wanted to get back to me. The me I was before this situation even entered my life. My life was successful, calm, and sweet.

# Part Two

# Chapter Fourteen

## Single but Smitten

As I entered into my newfound single season, dating was on my radar, but nothing serious. I was not open to relationships yet. I wanted to have a good time and enjoy it. If the company of a male was involved, that was cool too. I was not into all the meeting family and getting all comfortable with anyone. I was friendly, and having a great time. As I continued to enjoy myself, Rodrick would resurface at times. He realized the media platforms I did not block him on were open and would contact me that way. Outside of contacting me directly, he was also asking other people about me. When he did reach out, he said things like, "I know you still love me, and I still love you." He would randomly text me asking if I was going to be at a game or an event, and then he would say he was sorry, and that he was drunk. He would tell me that his daughter said "hello" and then he would go on to ask if we could work things out. I ignored these ridiculous messages. I felt like he thought I was stupid when he sent me those things. After all that we had been through, how could he possibly think we could be together? He got through with a call one time and was on the other end crying and saying he was sorry for everything. I wanted no part of it.

At the gym, I decided to get a trainer. I was serious about my fitness, and I wanted my body to be healthy and whole. My trainer was just the amount of seriousness I needed to get where I desired to go. The trainer and I became friends, and he invited some of us to his birthday party. It was fun to be out, laughing, and enjoying the time with like-minded people. We took pictures and had a great time. I was tagged in some of the images on Snapchat. Everyone loves the filters there. One of the other clients of the trainer noticed the tag and decided to add me. I knew of him because one night while I was talking with my trainer, he pulled up on us, his name was Brian. I was cool with adding him on Snapchat. After a while, Brian began chatting me up, giving me little compliments here and there. I appreciated the kindness. I would even flirt back at times, but I did not think much of it. One day though he saw a picture of me preparing to go out, and he boldly asked if he could take me out. At that point, I decided it would be okay if we exchanged numbers.

I appreciated this man wanting to take me out, but I was very particular about going out with people. This meant I would be seen with you. I needed to get to know a person before I went out with them. We began texting and chatting on the phone only at this point. I was interested in getting to know him better, as he was with me. Dating came naturally to me, but I was still particular about who I engaged with. The conversation with him was so good and entertaining. He was sweet and very consistent. I enjoyed that and at this point, those were the things that mattered to me. Relationship-wise though, I did not feel that for him. He continued to ask me to go on a date, and I continued to curve him. He was confident though, so he kept on asking.

I continued to enjoy our conversations and time, until one day I became very ill. I was sure I had contracted COVID. Brian called me, and I told him what was going on with me. A little while later, he arrived with medicine and food. He was so concerned, and he stayed and made sure I was not faint or having trouble breathing. I was very much comforted that he was there with me. I slept the whole time he was there, and he never tried anything sexual with me. My respect for him as a man began to increase. The next day, he showed up with even more supplies, stayed the night, and slept on the couch. I was a tad bit smitten by his kindness and gentleness.

# Chapter Fifteen

## Intuition

Although I was smitten by this young man, I was still not sold on going on a date with him. One night I woke up to a weird feeling in my nose. I jumped up extremely alert, and was like "What are you doing?" He was rubbing vapor rub under my nose and trying to make sure I was breathing. He caught me off guard. Afterwards I thought it was so funny that. We both were laughing. I had so much respect for him for being there for me. When I got better and regained my strength, I allowed him to come visit a little bit more. I started to open up to him more, letting him in. I told my mom about him, and she suggested I take him up on the date offer. She thought he was sweet, and it was about time I did. I decided to take her advice and agreed to go.

On our first date, we went to a local steakhouse. Brian was so funny, and we really enjoyed each other while out. The conversation went on and on. After that first date, we started to date on the regular. All of them were fun, and he would plan most of them. He would plan cute, unique things for us to do. On one Halloween we went to play paintball. I loved to do different things like that. We were also both foodies so he would find cool things to do that involved food, and we would head out. I loved the difference in what we were doing. Since we were spending so much time together, things between us began to speed up as well.

I dated before him, but there was something different about dating him. With others, I never felt like it was really going anywhere, but with him I did. I began to feel like this may be a good thing and may even be going to a good place. He had been so consistent about everything, I felt like he may just need a chance. I looked forward to what would happen next. We talked about our future a lot. I knew I had not given up on marriage and neither had he. We both wanted children as well. I also paid attention to my biological clock. I was getting older, and if I wanted a child the closing of that time frame was quickly approaching. I looked forward to being a mom.

Because we were both very clear on what we wanted to happen in the future, I trusted Brian a lot and I let my guard completely down. He also told me how open and honest he was with his ex. They communicated regularly because they had a valid reason to. They shared about their relationships for that reason, as well as to ensure that they never accidentally dated a friend of the other. They had chosen to never cross boundaries like that. I respected that as well. He told me his ex knew of me, and she thought I was cool. Due to us all attending the same college for undergrad mostly everyone knew of each other. I continued to respect the fact they never wanted to cause drama. She and I even happened to be friends on Facebook, which I had not noticed before.

After I realized she was my Facebook friend, I began to see her stories a whole lot more. I figured it was a coincidence, but I was still watching. She mentioned going on dates and spending time with someone. I felt like that was good for her. After seeing her mention this more and more, my intuition began to creep in. Something felt a bit strange in my spirit, but I told myself I would not pay attention to it too much and I would try not to care too much. I could not let it stress me out. This all could be just a coincidence. That was my thought process, until he came over one day and said he needed to go out of town without me.

# Chapter Sixteen

# A Mental Note

Since Rodrick, I had continued to take my mental health very seriously. I was maintaining my therapy sessions. I told my therapist how I felt and how he had left me to go out of town. She tried to ensure that I did not jump to conclusions. Brian was still texting me while he was gone. That gave me some confidence in him. He even called me. I watched his ex's story again and saw that she was at brunch with a guy. I could only really see the guy's shirt, but I knew it was the same shirt I had bought Brian. The image was a bit blurry, but I knew it was him. I began telling my friends my suspicions and they thought I was overreacting. As much as I wanted to believe that too, I knew it was him. He finally called me on Facetime, and I heard him fumbling and rummaging without being in the camera. I knew he was trying to take the shirt off. I asked him if he was taking it off, and he asked what I was even talking about. I truly hated to be made to feel like I was crazy and I was becoming angry. I told him not to play around with me while at the same time, I worked to maintain my cool.

Since my divorce, I made it a point not to appear crazy when it came to dating. I did not want to make any man think I was losing my head. I let the whole situation with the shirt go due to not wanting to act out prematurely. Once he returned back from out of town, nothing changed with us. He continued to be sweet. A little while later, he told me he needed to go out of town again. A best friend of his was getting his master's degree. I was not invited this time, because these were old friends of his, and I did know them so I would be out of place. I accepted that. In the midst of all of this happening, there were other strange occurrences. I did not understand what was going on, but I was sure he was playing games.

He soon left for the graduation trip. I saw in his ex's stories, that she was on a plane as well. That was quite a coincidence. He started texting me when he arrived but began complaining that service was rare and the texts would be few and far between. I continued to watch the story, and it was not long before her family tagged him in a video that they were in together. I did not say a word to him about what

I saw, but I blocked him from everything. After the graduation, he had already told me he was going on a business trip because one of his friends had passed away, and they were working on a project to keep the legacy going. He was heading to Florida. Once he was in Florida, we talked on the phone regularly with no interruptions.

I was storing up all of this information I had on him for later. When women act out prematurely, they give men time to figure out loopholes, and call them crazy. It is important to have all of the facts when presenting a case because it leaves them very little time to come up with anything. When he finally returned, he brought so many gifts. He was showering me with love. I noticed another young lady commented on a post he made. When I went and clicked on her page, I saw that this woman lived in Florida.

It truly hurt me to make all of these mental notes, but I had to. I needed to be credible and not feel insane. He began to wonder why he was blocked, and I revealed that I had seen the video from graduation. He explained that since this was his ex family, he thought it would be respectful to attend because they had all been family. He said he knew he should have told me. I mentally checked out with him. I was done. I tried to be more understanding because he sounded like he was really sorry, but it was hard for me. He went out and bought shoes, purses, and several other gifts for me. I was grateful, but I was not back to where we were. One night I woke up to use the bathroom, and when I wiped it was random blood. I was pregnant.

# Chapter Seventeen

## Case of the Ex

As anxious as I was, I had to wait until the store opened to get a test. It was early in the morning and I could not go back to sleep. I needed to know. Once the store opened, I rushed there and grabbed at least ten pregnancy tests. I ran back home to take them, and all of them were positive. I could not believe it. I began reaching out to a few of my friends to see if I was seeing all of this right. I asked them if they saw the same line I saw. They all assured me that they did. I got so excited. I happened to be home by myself that morning because Brian had to work late so he stayed at home that night. I called him, and he was so sleepy on the phone. I told him I had some news and I could not hold it any longer. He heard me, and he told me he was happy. Even though he was still asleep, he sounded so excited. It was a fast conversation, but I was happy to hear that he was as happy as I was. He told me he would call me when he woke up.

We continued to talk about the baby. We found out on a Friday, so he came right over for the weekend. I was able to see then that he was happy. We continued as normal and worked on our relationship. That Monday, I had an appointment scheduled to confirm everything. I was confident I was pregnant, but it was time to go ahead and get under a doctor. Once we were at the doctor they performed a blood test and confirmed my pregnancy. After that, I needed an appointment, but I would have to wait to be seen. While waiting, I began to notice I was bleeding again, so I rushed to an ultrasound center. I felt like I was miscarrying, and I didn't even know if I was pregnant anymore. They told me that everything was normal, and sometimes older blood in the lining of the uterus could leave the body. I felt reassured after that.

Brian was there with me every step of the way. He let me know early on that he wanted to be a part of the journey. He was buying me so many things like vitamins, prune juice, and anything else I needed. He was attentive to my needs, and I felt blessed to have that. He was attending appointments with me. Everything was going well. We continued to go on our dates to laugh and enjoy each other's company. The quality time was important to me. One night we were on a date and somehow his ex arrived at the restaurant. We were sitting and had already ordered. All of a sudden Brian said he needed to use the restroom. I noticed an exchange between them, but I had no idea what was said exactly, I just heard him say, "Okay, Okay." He came back and sat down. The situation was so awkward. She left while he was returning to his seat. I assumed she must have seen his car in the parking lot.

Once Brian sat back down, something was different about him. He seemed guilty about something and sad. The vibe was very much off, and I hated it. I went ahead and asked him what was going on and what she had wanted, but he brushed it off. I felt that the whole situation was just petty and caddy. I hated that our date night was ruined because I was looking forward to eating and enjoying time with him. I finally asked if he was ready to go. He went ahead and took me home. He told me that night, that he told his ex I was pregnant. I told him that since I was pregnant, there was no way I was going to deal with drama. He went on to tell me that he understood, but she was upset and mad about it. At that point, I knew she had to have thought they were going to work things out. I tried to remain calm about all of this, but it was truly upsetting me. It was not long after this that I received a message from a mutual friend of mine and his ex, letting me know that Brian's ex wanted my number so she could talk to me.

# Chapter Eighteen

## Choose

I was upset. Not because his ex wanted to speak with me, but because it was now evident that people who I did not tell, knew I was pregnant. I did not like that at all. I had not announced my pregnancy yet. I knew she knew I was pregnant, and I am guessing this warranted a conversation. I told the friend to go ahead and give her my number. She called and the information about the status of her and Brian just rolled off her tongue. She told me that they were often together, even more than I thought. She said they took trips together and were supposed to be working things out. They did not actually go on any dates, but she wasted no time telling me she could have him when she wanted him, and however she wanted him. The ball was in her court. They were not serious, but they still dealt with each other.

This was all so heartbreaking to hear. Brian had lied to me for so long. He was trying to please everyone. He could not be loyal to me because he needed to make her happy. I sat down with him and let him know I knew everything, and I was hurt. He told me he wanted to do better, and he wanted to be with me. He said he wanted us to be a family. I was hurting, but very emotional, so I wanted to believe him. I truly cared for him, and I would have liked for us to be a family as well, but I knew we could not as long as all of this was going on.

My birthday was coming, and as usual, he wanted to take me out to eat. I enjoyed our dates, so I looked forward to it. As we were riding to the restaurant, a call kept coming through. I asked if it was his ex because I noticed the familiarity of the number. He told me it was not her, and that he would call them back later. I encouraged him to go ahead and answer because the phone kept ringing. He refused to answer it. As we were sitting down preparing to order, his ex began to text me. She asked if I was with him. I let him know what was going on, and he told me he did not care if I told her or not. I told her I was. She then began texting us both in a group chat. She was sending images, and screenshots, proving that they were still together. She even claimed that they were in an actual relationship. At this point, I was so done.

I let Brian know that night, that he needed to choose. I told him that if I needed to raise my baby on my own, I was willing to do so. I was becoming stressed, and this was not healthy for the baby. This was drama and I did not need it in my life. It was evident that what I thought we had, we did not have. At this point, I knew I had to come to terms with that. I told him something needed to change so I could have peace. I never responded to the group messages, and neither did he. I asked him what he wanted to do. He once again responded that he wanted it to work with us. He wanted to focus on us. I was trying my best not to get upset. Brian needed to be a man and handle this. This woman did not know me, and I wanted no part of this. I was in the middle of whatever they had, which had nothing to do with me. A part of me still wanted to make it work, but I know it was all of the emotions and hormones. That night he stayed over with promises to work on us.

# Chapter Nineteen

## Lies

As time progressed, Brian continued to do what an expecting father does. He showed up and took me to appointments. We were entering the month of May. He was still at my house most days, and when he was not there, we would talk on the phone consistently. Everything was going quite fine. One night, he called to let me know he was going out with friends. I figured since he had been doing so great with me, he deserved a break. I was watching Snapchat later that night though, and I noticed that his friends were drunk. They were having a great time, but the drunkenness was to the point that one friend had to vomit on the side of the road. They were sloppy. I began to be concerned about Brian.

I called his phone, and he would not answer. Normally he at least checked in to let me know he made it home or he came to my house. There was no word from him at all this particular night. At this point, I needed to know that he was okay, so I decided to drive over to his home to make sure. He still would not answer at all. I knew something was off. Once I arrived, I found his car was not there. Things were becoming very strange. I remembered him telling me about an incident where he once lived with his ex, and because I knew what I felt in my heart, I went over there. I was not sure which apartment it was, but I knew I would know his car. As I drove through the complex and turned a corner, there he was.

People can say a ton of things, but one thing about intuition, it is real. I felt like such an idiot. I believed this man when he told me he wanted to work on us, that he wanted me to trust him, and that he wanted us to be a whole family. I was heartbroken. I wanted to take my bat from the trunk and burst all of his windows. I began to call him frantically. I was so angry that he had played me. The anger permeated me, and I knew if I did anything more I was going to jail. I was ready for someone to hurt just like me. I knew I was pregnant and I could not go to jail. I called my mom and she was able to talk me off the ledge. I finally started the drive home.

I stayed up all night. The pregnancy made it way more emotional than it should have been. I knew that before I would not have cared that much. I had worked to not let anyone get to me emotionally. My friend instructed me to ask him where he had been once he called. Once he did call, he started to explain that he had just woken up. I told him that I had called so much because I knew he and his friends were drunk. He went on to say he went home and fell asleep. I then went on to tell him, that he was not home, because I had driven by. He then changed his story and stated he was actually at his homeboy's house. After the second lie, I went on to tell him exactly where he was. I allowed him two chances to tell the truth. I started to cry, as I told him I was so tired of him playing games with me. After that, I ended the call.

That afternoon I had a braid appointment. As I sat there and talked to my braider about the situation, he continued to text and apologize. I was so bothered by it all. I even called my therapist to discuss it. That night I did not sleep well either. The day after the braid appointment, I had to go to work. While working, he continued to call and apologize even more. He kept saying that nothing was going on, but how could I believe him after all that had happened? He told me he only went over there to sleep which made no sense because there were multiple places he could have slept. He kept trying to convince me. I continued to work on my client and tried to press through the day. Suddenly I felt as if I was peeing on myself. I thought this was normal though, and just something pregnant women went through at times. I finished the last twist on my client's hair and sat her under the dryer. I went into the bathroom and saw a ton of water coming from my body. I was going into labor.

# Chapter Twenty

## Prayers

I went into panic mode. I began googling what was happening to me. I called Brian and told him, but he felt that I was okay, and maybe I was overreacting. I knew I wasn't and I needed to go get help. I explained to my client and she understood and agreed with me that I needed to go get help. I left work and headed to the doctor's office, which happened to be inside the hospital. I explained the situation, and the entire office went into panic. I had no idea what was happening, or what any of this meant. I was so unclear and lost. They took me into the back to perform an ultrasound and determined there was no longer any fluid in my body to protect my baby. My water had broken, just as I thought. I was devastated.

The ultrasound tech left the room and said I needed to go to the hospital. When I arrived at the hospital they sat me down and explained things. They said I needed to listen.

They went on to tell me that my baby was preparing to enter the world, and I would need to prepare to give birth. I was speechless, because also according to them I had not dilated at all. How was I going to give birth? I was only twenty-one weeks, and my baby would not survive at this rate. I lost it completely after this. I began to cry hysterically. Everyone in the room felt my pain. The doctor hugged me and attempted to comfort me. My heart was breaking in two. I kept asking what I could do to change this. I needed to save my baby. They told me that in ten days time, I should be having my baby girl. They explained that by the way she was headdown, she was certainly ready to come. They admitted me into a room, to prepare to give birth.

I called my mom and told her what was happening. She tried to be strong for me. I was telling her that her first grandchild was not going to make it, and she was hurting as well. I could hear it in her voice. Brian arrived at the hospital, and he was looking nervous and scared. He was crying, and holding my hand, telling me how sorry he was. After I was able to calm down a little I began canceling client appointments. My mom arrived later, and we all just sat there. My doctor came back in and told me the Intensive Care Unit doctor would be coming in to explain some things. All

I could think about was how tiny my baby was at this time. If she came into this world, I would be so distraught and afraid.

When the ICU doctor arrived, he began to explain things to me concerning what would happen after I gave birth. He was quite blunt and told me this was best for me: a stillbirth. He said I did not want my baby to come into this world with multiple complications including cerebral palsy. He kept saying over and over how I did not want a baby like this. He told me most of my days would be spent at the doctor. I did not want to hear any of this. My doctor was able to see the affect his comments were having on me, so she tapped him, and let him know that was enough. One night a nurse came in, and I asked her what could I do to change my situation. She told me that she did not know if I was religious or not, but she had witnessed many miracles in that hospital, and I needed to call on the God I serve to help me. I stopped to think about what she said, and I determined that she was right. I began to pray and pray, and as days went by I still had not dilatated, and therefore could not give birth.

# Chapter Twenty-One

## Counting Weeks

Google became my best friend while in the hospital. I googled everything and most importantly looked for other women who had experienced this. There was one woman who had experienced this exact same thing at eighteen weeks. She drank a ton of water in an effort to restore the baby's fluid that was lost. I was all over YouTube looking for answers. I began drinking water, hoping my situation would change. I soon realized this was probably not helping because my amniotic fluid would come out when I used the restroom. I was grateful to have my mom there with me almost every day. After two days, I was told I could go home. I had never dilated, but they told me I could go home and come back when the contractions started. They gave me medication to combat any infection that may occur. After getting all of these instructions, I went home.

My mom moved in with me for the duration, because I could not move much at all. Brian came, brought food, and also helped my mom with my needs. He also stayed around and helped when my mom needed to go home. They were able to work out a schedule and alternate their care for me. During this time, after all of my research, I realized that if I made it to twenty- two weeks, there was a slight chance my baby could live. My doctor was calling regularly to check on me, but nothing was happening. I was praying daily that my baby did not die inside of me. I would have nightmares that I was in labor with her. I was so scared, and dilation was still not happening. After a while the hospital stepped in with a few options for me. I needed more care at this point. They had the care available locally, or I could go to Birmingham. Birmingham seemed to specialize in my situation, so I decided to go there. My mom drove me there to begin the process.

At this point, I was doing whatever needed to be done to save my baby. I was checked into the hospital, and they began scans. I was told I was still running the risk of issues. They explained that my baby had a hole in her heart. This alarmed me. Days went by, and my baby still never came. My mom came to the hospital almost every day. I appreciated my parents so much. They were truly standing by me in this difficult time. The support was needed. Brian came once a week, and stayed a full day when he came. I was trying to make the best out of my situation, but being in the hospital was becoming so overwhelming. The hospital staff was very thorough and although I appreciated this, it became exhausting. They checked her heart rate all the time, and if it ever started to increase or decrease, they told me they would need to take her. I prayed that this did not happen. They checked her around the clock. Friends came to visit, as well as cousins, and other family members. It was good to see familiar faces. I also took a break from social media during this time. It was summer, and people were having fun, and living. This became so depressing for me. Television and streaming services were my companions.

As time progressed my optimism grew. I knew as my baby grew inside me she was becoming more viable. At twenty- three weeks, I knew she could make it. I started shopping online for things she may need. As the weeks continued to fly by, I was hopeful. I started researching and learning more about my baby. The days in the hospital got harder and harder. They would come to check on us extremely early in the morning. Right after the morning check there was breakfast, cleaning, and then the doctor had to do his rounds. There was very little rest for me. I was on the brink of losing it with the nurses, doctors, custodians, and all. I had to tell them I needed a mental break. Eventually they understood, so they put a note on my door at certain times asking people not to bother me. I appreciated that. I think they understood I had been there so long, and they decided to respect and honor my request. I ended up having to take sleeping pills nightly to go to sleep. By the grace of God, I was still getting my regular therapy sessions via Zoom. My therapist went through the entire journey with me. Being able to be consistent helped me manage being in the hospital. I was journaling my feelings and expressing myself. I was grateful for the outlet. My local doctor called to check on me and was shocked that I was still pregnant. Around this time, things began to get painful. I was so irritated, and at this point, I was going off on people.

# Chapter Twenty-Two

# Mom

I came to the realization that my baby was sitting on my pelvis. It hurt so bad, I was almost in tears. There were other women on the floor experiencing things as well. Some of them were having mental meltdowns. It was a combination of not knowing the outcome of their situation and being stuck in the hospital cut off from civilization. We were all so bothered. I could hear the screaming sometimes coming from down the hall. They were screams of frustration. Being able to hold it together a bit better (due to my therapist) I was asked to speak to some of the women as a form of encouragement. There was so much going on, and I was ready to go home with my baby.

Weeks went by, and I was now in the 27th week of pregnancy. One night, I began to have contractions. They hurt so badly. My mom was there, and she began to explain what was happening. When the doctors came in, they told me I was contracting, but not well enough to give birth. I had been brought down to the delivery room by then, thinking it was time, but it was not. Brian was there, along with my mother and Godmother, but this was just a false alarm. Two days went by, and it began to happen again, but this time it was time. I told Brian what was happening, but he didn't leave in enough time to make the delivery. I was okay with that, because my mom and Godmother were there, and I was happy to be having my baby. I was about to give birth. As we waited for the doctor to come in, we were all laughing at something, and I was laughing really hard. The nurse came in first and began searching for the baby's heartbeat. She could not find it. I was becoming alarmed, and she called the doctor in to check. When they discovered the heartbeat, it was near my vagina, and she was puzzled as to why. When she moved the covers back, she discovered my baby was already out of my body lying on the sheets.

She was so quiet. The doctor began to rub my babies back, and then I heard her. She was fine. She pressed a button, and all of the doctors came in. They allowed me to see her very quickly and we were able to snap a few pics. Once that was done, they took her out immediately. They told me I could see her again in two hours. I was so happy. My baby was here and she was healthy. I knew in that moment that God truly smiled on me. Brian arrived shortly after.

For the next eight weeks my baby remained in the hospital, growing, and preparing for the day she would come home. I always wanted to be close to her, so I stayed at the McDonald's House the hospital provided for parents of children with various appointments or premature babies. It was absolutely free, and sort of like a hotel. They offered meals and all. I tried my best to focus while there, but I was depressed because my baby was not well, and most days I felt all alone in this. I hated leaving the hospital after a visit with her. On weekends I would go back home to prep the nursery and prepare for my baby. As much as I wanted her home, I knew it would happen soon enough.

# Chapter Twenty-Three

## No Help

My focus was on my baby coming home. I needed everything to be as perfect as possible for her. Brian came and assisted with putting her crib together. I appreciated it. He and I had ended things, and he had moved on. There was never any closure with us, I kind of figured he went back to his ex which always seemed to be the underlying plan. With my healing from that, and my baby's condition there were times I still felt like I was in this alone. That is when the depression sunk in. So much was happening during this time, and on-top of it all the bills were piling up. I had not worked in a while and my savings had significantly decreased. I asked Brian to help me with some things, but of course, he was not able to do anything concerning bills. He did purchase food for me while I was staying at the McDonald's House.

The hospital informed me they had resources to assist with bills. I was able to apply for that and I was awarded. Some of my clients even reached out and assisted with whatever I needed. God was truly smiling on me. I was grateful to get a handle on the bills so I could focus on my baby. It was mentally exhausting some days as I sat back and just waited on her progress. There was an update each day, and I was grateful for that. She was progressing so well, and finally it was time for her to come home. I was overjoyed and so grateful.

Once we were home, I worked on learning my baby's routines. She did not cry a lot, and she was such a sweet baby. I was with her all day and night, and Brian would come over and help out in the mornings. There was so much to do during the day, like errands, and then at night I had to stay up and watch her, so I was not getting much sleep at all. At the most, I was averaging about two hours of sleep per day. Unfortunately, there was no overnight help for me. The more the lack of sleep got to me, I felt my postpartum depression set in. One day while Brian was with the baby, I sat on the toilet and cried. After crying many tears, I went to Brian and asked for his help. I told him how I was feeling, how tired I was, and how I needed more help. Brian looked at me and told me that he had already explained what he could do. In that moment, I realized there was no help.

# Part Three

# Chapter Twenty-Four

## Healing Time

It was time for me to put on my big girl panties and do this. Brian explained his boundaries to me as far as where we stood, and what he could and could not do for me. I was fine with it all. I had begun building my village. My family and friends were ready and willing to step in and help me as I prepared to go back to work. My Godmother agreed to keep my baby during the day until she became ready for daycare. My little family needed support, and I was ready to get back out there. We established our routine, and things became better for me mentally. I felt so much better, and so much more under control.

Co-parenting, which was still a bit foreign to me, was a chore. There was always another layer to deal with soon after I was still getting over my traumatic hospital stay. When people live separate lives with a child in common, it can be hard because you can't control what they do on their own time, or how it will affect your routine. I did not realize how much adjusting I needed to be able to process certain things that were happening so fast. My therapist reminded me that I never got a break, or any relaxation time during any of this. So, it was natural that I felt strained with so much anxiety about all that was happening. I really just needed a moment to heal before so many changes, and adjustments piled up.

I knew my therapist was amazing, but I also wanted to maintain my relationship with God. I began to build my relationship with Him and seek healing through Him. I began to utilize affirmations that I recited before starting my day. I needed to remind myself that I could do all things. I had to be strong for my baby more than anything. I also knew my business needed me. As I focused on my mental health, God, and my baby, I was able to gain the strength to work on my business and my branding. I was so proud of how everything began to fall into place. I had never felt better. I trusted God so much, and I was happier than I had been in a while, and at the six-month mark, Brian and I agreed it was time for daycare.

# Chapter Twenty-Five

# Healed and Whole

Today, co-parenting is not so much a chore. We have learned our rhythm and we stick to the plan. There are times when I become a bit irritated, but I have learned to not choose violence, but peace, because at the end of the day, my daughter has her father in her life, and that matters most. We solely speak as it pertains to our daughter. There is no need to cross boundaries or become involved in each other's personal business. We share something way more special than that, so it is easy to put our feelings aside and focus on her. The drama-free life I have is a blessing, and I don't take it for granted.

I am no longer allowing my emotions to consume me in any way. I love being able to put my baby first. I have learned to trust God through it all. What He has done for me in this process is unmatched. From start to finish I know He was there, and He has still been present in all that I do now. I want other mothers to know there is never anything too hard for God, never a relationship He cannot mend and make right. I am so grateful that I know that now, and I can live in my truth, and be content and happy.

I love not being angry anymore. Even when I have grounds to be angry, there is no sense in it, and there is no sense in trying to retaliate either. I let things glide off me and I love it. It is not that I am a pushover by any means, but always ask yourself if it is worth addressing, and be mindful of how you address things. Be sure you are not lashing out with emotion rather than reason. Say what needs to be said only and move on and let God handle it. God will fight your battles as long as they are legitimate and not petty. I am a witness to this and I always end up on top.

People often ask me, how I move on so fast from people and situations. I would like to share something my mother would always say to me: NEXT! You can not dwell on what hurt you. Move on! As harsh as it sounds, you have to. God will always give you better. So maybe your next season has bigger blessings in it and better friendships and relationships. There's always something better in your next chapter. Another piece of wisdom my mom shares with me is to never think that God won't handle the people who hurt you. He will, in his own time. They will reap what they sow. In the meantime, you have to keep looking forward and trust in the future that God has for you.

Get a therapist. I have no regrets about bringing therapy into my life. I love my friends and family because they pray for me, but I know that my therapist has been pivotal to my growth. Sometimes you need reason and science, and even more Jesus to make things make sense. Don't shy away from that or allow stigmas to stop you. Get the help you need. Remember it does not matter what you encounter, or who you encounter it with, you can still make it. These are all just people, and when you allow them to take you to places of deep anger, you are making them more than that. Remember you cannot control the actions of others, only you. You are accountable for you. Therapy will give you that clarity, and let you know "why."

To anyone that's reading that has dealt with the situations I have detailed, I am truly sorry. We have to call things as they are when we see it. Once you identify the signs, believe them for who they are, and leave immediately. You cannot fix people. People will lie, manipulate, and mentally abuse you. They can truly be energy drainers. It's them and not you.

Before having children, marry the person that you are equally yoked with so that you can be well supported throughout the pregnancy and avoid being a single mother. Around the time I became pregnant I was okay with having a child out of wedlock due to my divorce. Marriage was nowhere near my mind. I am not making an excuse for what I went through, as I didn't deserve it, but because I did things my way, and not God's way, there were consequences. I received a great blessing, but lessons came with it. God's way is always better. He has His commandments for a reason. Trust Him and His timing with your life. Believe the scripture, "For I know the plans I have for you says the Lord. They are plans for good and not for disaster, to give you a future and a hope." Jeremiah 29:11. May God be with each of you.

# Acknowledgements

## My Village

My parents, Deborah and Darrell, my stepfather Luthus, and my Godparents, Violet and Freddie, thank you for always being by my side throughout my life. During every tough time in my life, you all were always there. I love y'all!

Mom, thank you for being the best mother ever. Throughout my entire life you have always shown up. Because of you, I am who I am. Because of you, I know how to be the best mother to my daughter. Thank you for being my biggest cheerleader.

Dad, you have been the best dad a girl could have. You have pushed me to my full potential in life. You're one of the reasons for my go-getter mentality. Thank you for being there.

Bonus dad, and Godparents, thank you for always being by my side throughout my life. During every tough time in my life you all were always there. I love yall.

## My Extended Village

My Edge-2-Edge Salon Family: Keisha, Tiffany, and Fredche

My best friend: Marissa

My friend and confidante: Dr. Jonelle

Thank you all for our many night talks, advice, prayers, and keeping your arms wrapped around me. Brunch has always been cute, but you ladies have always been ready to ride at dawn and send up prayers too. I am thankful for you ladies!

# About the Author

Jasmine Wright, originally from Auburn, Alabama, is a proud graduate of Opelika High School in Opelika, Alabama. She furthered her education at THEE Alabama State University, where she earned a Bachelor of Science in Criminal Justice, graduating Cum Laude. During her time at Alabama State, Jasmine was an active member of Kappa Phi Chapter of the Alpha Kappa Psi Business Fraternity and the House Arrest 2 Championship Dance Team Inc. Chapter 8.

In addition to her academic achievements, Jasmine is also a licensed cosmetologist and a certified dance fitness instructor. Her passion for dance and beauty, combined with her commitment to empowering others, reflects her multifaceted talents and interests.

Jasmine's biggest goal in life is to accomplish all of the dreams that God has placed inside of her and to inspire as many women as she can to be the best versions of themselves. She is also dedicated to being the best mother she can be to her daughter, Khori.

In recognition of her outstanding contributions to the community and her role as a positive influence for young women, Jasmine was awarded the Black Girl Excellence Lighthouse Award. This accolade highlights her commitment to excellence and her unwavering dedication to uplifting others.

# *Contact the Author*

**Email:** Jnicoleandko@gmail.com

**YouTube:** Jnicoleandko

**Facebook:** J.Nicole & ko

**Instagram:** Jnicole.ko

**Website:** www.jnicoleandko.com